MIDFIELD HEROES

Jonny Zucker

Badger Publishing Limited
Oldmedow Road,
Hardwick Industrial Estate,
King's Lynn PE30 4JJ
Telephone: 01438 791037

www.badgerlearning.co.uk

2 4 6 8 10 9 7 5 3 1

Midfield Heroes ISBN 978-1-78464-014-9

Publisher: Susan Ross
Senior Editor: Danny Pearson
Publishing Assistant: Claire Morgan
Designer: Fiona Grant
Series Consultant: Dee Reid

Photos: Cover Image: Caiaimage/REX
Page 5: Manchester City Football Club
Page 6: Graham Chadwick/Daily Mail/REX
Page 7: © WENN Ltd/Alamy
Page 8: Kieran McManus/BPI/REX
Page 11: Mark Large/Associated Newspa/REX
Page 12: Andy Hooper/Daily Mail/REX
Page 13: Eddie Keogh/REX
Page 15: © Action Plus Sports Images/Alamy
Page 16: © Action Plus Sports Images/Alamy
Page 17: © ZUMA Press, Inc./Alamy
Page 18: © dpa picture alliance/Alamy
Page 19: © epa european pressphoto agency b.v./A
Page 20: Robin Hume/REX
Page 21: © Aflo Co. Ltd./Alamy
Page 22: © wareham.nl (sport)/Alamy
Page 23: © epa european pressphoto agency b.v./Alamy
Page 24: © Aflo Co. Ltd./Alamy
Page 25: © ZUMA Press, Inc./Alamy
Page 26: © Action Plus Sports Images/Alamy
Page 27: © Associated Sports Photography/Alamy
Page 28: © Associated Sports Photography/Alamy
Page 29: © Aflo Co. Ltd./Alamy
Page 30: © Action Plus Sports Images/Alamy

Attempts to contact all copyright holders have been made.
If any omitted would care to contact Badger Learning, we will be happy to make appropriate arrangements.

MIDFIELD HEROES

Contents

Vocabulary

assists   opposition

diagonal   overall

encourages   position

incredible   youngest

1. Goal getters

Do you like playing football?

What position do you like to play?

Lots of people like to play striker. They like to score goals.

But midfielders score goals too.

When Manchester City won the Premier League in 2014, their midfield player, Yaya Touré, scored an incredible 22 goals.

In a match against Aston Villa near the end of the 2014 season, Touré ran the length of the pitch and then scored. This goal was a giant step towards Manchester City winning the title.

Which midfield player in the Premier League has the best overall record for scoring goals?

Name	Club	Games played	Goals scored	Average goals per match
Rafael van der Vaart	Tottenham	63	24	0.38

Which midfield player in the Premier League had the highest transfer fee?

Name	Club	Transfer to	Fee
Gareth Bale	Tottenham	Real Madrid	£85.3 million

Bale's best goal in the 2013/14 season

Near the end of the season, Bale scored an incredible solo goal against Barcelona.

Picking the ball up in his own half, his speed and strength took him right into the Barcelona penalty area where he slotted the ball home.

2. Assists

What is an assist?

An assist is when one player helps another player just before a goal is scored.

What kind of assists are there?
- a corner
- a free kick
- a header
- a pass

Who is the Premier League's number one assist champion?

Name	Club	Assists
Ryan Giggs	**Manchester United**	130

Some clubs have midfield players who provide lots of assists.

Club	Players
Arsenal	**Mesut Ozil** **Aaron Ramsey** **Santi Cazorla** **Alex Oxlade-Chamberlain** **Mikel Arteta**

Question: What is the sign of a great team player?

Answer: A player who scores lots of goals and provides lots of assists.

Name	Position	Club	Season	Goals	Assists
Cristiano Ronaldo	**Midfield**	**Real Madrid**	**2013/ 2014**	50	14

Ronaldo's free kick speed is over 30 metres per second.

3. Midfield captains

Question: Do midfield players make good captains?

Answer: Yes!

When	Match	Half time score
2005 Champions League Final	**Liverpool vs AC Milan**	**AC Milan: 3 Liverpool: 0**

Liverpool looked to be down and out.

But then in the second half, Steven Gerrard, Liverpool's midfield captain, drove them forwards.

He scored one goal and assisted in two more. At full time it was 3-3 and Liverpool went on to win 3-2 on penalties.

Roy Keane was Manchester United's midfield captain from 1997 to 2005. He scored many times for them.

But he got very angry if he thought other members of the team were not playing their best.

Keane also got cross with the opposition. He could be very aggressive on the pitch and he was often given a red or yellow card.

Name	Club	Red cards	Yellow cards
Roy Keane	**Manchester United**	7	69

4. Start young

Some midfield players start young.

Name	First played for Southampton Academy	First played for Southampton	First played for England
Adam Lallana	**aged 12**	**aged 18**	**aged 25**

Adam Lallana

- 2009/2010 season: scored 20 goals

- 2010/2011: League One Team of the Year
  scored 11 goals

- 2014: named Southampton Fans' 'Player of the Year'

- 2014: one of six players on the Professional Players'
  'Player of the Year' list

Midfield player: Cesc Fabregas

- Aged 10: Signed for Barcelona Youth Academy

- Aged 16: Joined Arsenal

- Aged 16: Arsenal's youngest ever first team player

- Aged 17: Arsenal's youngest ever goal scorer in a league game

Since returning to Barcelona in 2011, Fabregas had a pretty amazing record.

Name	Club	League goals	Cup goals	Europe goals
Cesc Fabregas	Barcelona	28	14	13

Not a bad scoring record for a midfield player!

He moved to Chelsea Football Club in 2014.

5. Passing kings

The job of the midfield player is to pass the ball on to the forwards.

Question: Who is the world's best midfield passer of a football?
Answer: Xabi Alonso

Xabi has played for Liverpool, Real Madrid and Spain. His passes are very accurate.

His special move is the long diagonal pass.

Midfield player David Beckham was also a world-class passer of the ball.

He tried passes that no one else would try.

His manager, Sir Alex Ferguson, nicknamed Beckham's long passes 'Hollywood' balls.

The midfield player Xavier Hernandez (nickname Xavi) is brilliant at the short passing style of play used by Barcelona and Spain.

This style is called 'tiki-taka'. Xavi's skill at one-touch passing is amazing. He can also make perfect passes when he is in very tight spaces.

WOW! facts

Xavi often makes as many passes as four of the opposition side put together!

Holland's Wesley Sneijder is brilliant at passing. But what makes him stand out is that he can make perfect passes with both feet!

This makes life very difficult for the defenders facing him.

6. Holding things back

Not all midfielders try to score. Some play in a 'holding' or defensive style.

Arsenal's Mathieu Flamini encourages his team-mates to go forwards while he hangs back. If the opposition get the ball and head for the goal, Flamini is waiting for them.

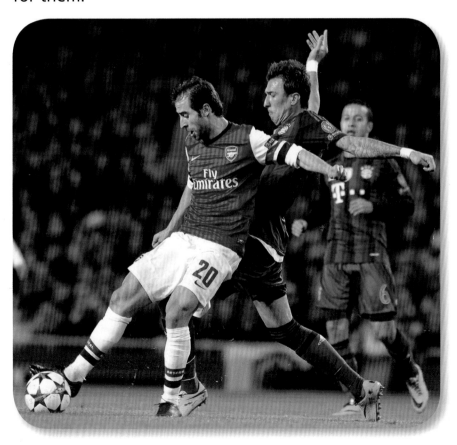

Tackling is a vital skill for midfielders who hold back.

Most people think that the best tackler is Bastian Schweinsteiger of Bayern Munich.

What is so good about Schweinsteiger?
- very strong
- accurate in the tackle
- doesn't give away too many free kicks

Gareth Barry (from Aston Villa, Manchester City and Everton) is brilliant at holding the ball.

He does this to allow his team-mates to get forward before passing to them.

He has one of the best passing accuracy rates in the world. That's why he's played for England over 50 times.

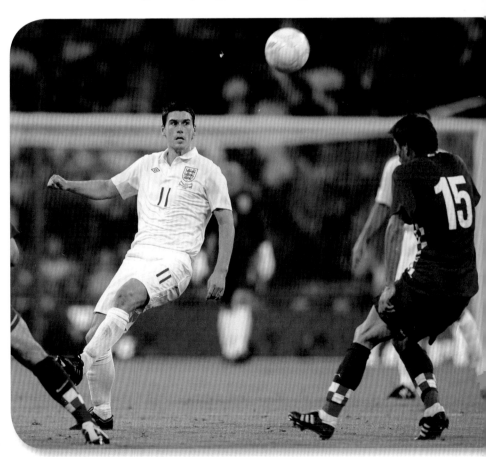

Another midfield player who is brilliant at holding the ball is Paul Pogba.

He is French but plays for the Italian side Juventus.

Pogba likes to play in front of the line of defence. He is great at mopping up attacks and beginning counter-attacks.

7. The greatest

Who is the world's best midfield player?

Some people would say that Zinedine Zidane (nickname Zizou) of France was the best.

What were his skills?

- brilliant dribbling
- perfect passing
- accurate shooting

Zizou could also control a ball at any angle and at any height.

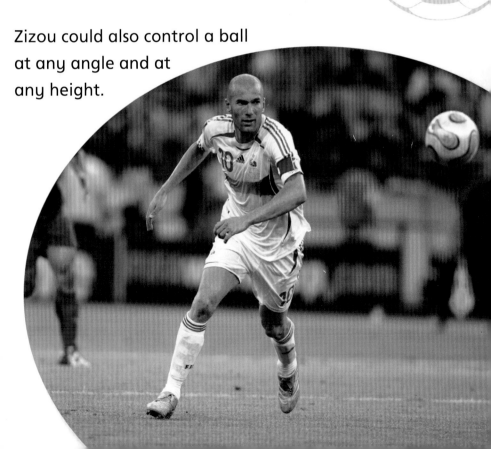

Other people would say that the world's best midfield player was Diego Maradona of Argentina.

What were his skills?
- incredible speed
- close ball control
- amazing dribbling

In the 1986 World Cup Final he dribbled the ball 60 metres, past five England players, to score one of the most famous goals of all time.

Andrés Iniesta of Spain and Barcelona is another great midfield player.

His passing and his dribbling are fantastic. Iniesta has won the Champions League with Barcelona three times.

He also scored Spain's winning goal against Holland in the 2010 World Cup Final.

The Brazilian player Neymar started his career at Santo
like the great Pelé. Today he plays for Barcelona.

His dribbling skills and speed make him almost impossibl
to tackle and he scores great goals every season.

WOW!facts

Ronaldinho has said that his
fellow Brazilian, Neymar, will be
the 'best player in the world'.

Questions

Who did Yaya Touré play for in the Premier League 2014 season? *(page 5)*

How much did it cost Real Madrid to buy Gareth Bale? *(page 7)*

What was the half time score in the 2005 Champions League Final? *(page 11)*

In what year did Cesc Fabregas move to Chelsea? *(page 18)*

What country is Diego Maradona from? *(page 28)*

In which World Cup Final did Andrés Iniesta score the winning goal? *(page 29)*

Index